ENERGY FILES

NUCLEAR

Steve Parker

Heinemann
LIBRARY

CONTENTS

Still and silent, the vast dome of a nuclear power station hides the equipment from view, and helps to contain the results of an accident.

Our nuclear power units travel to other worlds, including the Moon, and even beyond the Sun and planets, in deep-space probes.

ENERGY FILES

NUCLEAR

ENERGY FILES – NUCLEAR
was produced by

David West 🏃 Children's Books
7 Princeton Court
55 Felsham Road
London SW15 1AZ

Editor: James Pickering
Picture Research: Carlotta Cooper

First published in Great Britain in 2002 by
Heinemann Library, Halley Court, Jordan Hill,
Oxford OX2 8EJ, a division of Reed Educational
and Professional Publishing Limited.

OXFORD MELBOURNE AUCKLAND
JOHANNESBURG BLANTYRE GABORONE
IBADAN PORTSMOUTH (NH) USA CHICAGO

06 05 04 03 02
10 9 8 7 6 5 4 3 2 1

ISBN 0 431 15573 9 (HB)
ISBN 0 431 15580 1 (PB)

British Library Cataloguing in Publication Data

Parker, Steve, 1952 -
Nuclear power. - (Energy files)
1. Nuclear energy - Juvenile literature
I. Title
333.7'924

PHOTO CREDITS :
Abbreviations: t-top, m-middle, b-bottom, r-right,
l-left, c-centre.

Front cover ml & b - Corbis Images, mr, 5b & 21 -
(CH. Zuber) Still Pictures. 3, 4tr, 4-5b & 25b, 8bl,
12t, 20bm, 23ml, 24br, 25tr, 26br - Corbis Images.
5tr & 24-25 (Larsen), 17tr (Gleizes) - Greenpeace.
6bl, 7bl, 9br - Mary Evans Picture Library. 6-7t,
22m, 28bl, 30tl (Jecko Vassilev), 10tr (Marek
Libersky), 11tl (Hartmut Schwarzbach), 11br, 16b -
(Klaus Andrews), 12mr, 19tr, 29tr (Sabine Vielmo),
15tr, 22bl, 22-23 (Thomas Raupach), 16tr (Andre
Maslennikov), 16m (Daniel Dancer), 21br (Peter
Frischmuth), 28br (Savran), 30mr (Jean-François
Mutzig) - Still Pictures 7br, 8-9t, 15bl, 18-19t & b,
19tl, 20mr & b, 29bl - Katz/FSP. 12b, 18bl, 21tr,
24bl - Rex Features. 13tr, 14bl, 22br, 28-29t -
Spectrum Colour Library. 26-27, 27tr, bl & br -
EFDA - JET.

Printed and bound in Italy

*An explanation of difficult words can be
found in the glossary on page 31.*

INTRODUCTION

Nuclear energy is one of our most mysterious energy sources, and difficult for people to understand. It also creates the hottest arguments that sometimes explode in anger. Nuclear energy is the power locked up in the tiniest, most common objects in the entire Universe – atoms. But obtaining this energy in a useful form is a very high-tech process with many risks and hazards. Will nuclear power save our world, or destroy it?

Protesters risk their lives to demonstrate against the use of nuclear power – which, in this case, propels an icebreaker ship.

If nuclear energy is released all at once, out of control, the result is an explosion of unimagined power. It can destroy a whole city in five seconds.

ACTION IN THE ATOM

Everything in the Universe is made of tiny particles called atoms. They are too small to see. But some types give off energy that we can harness and use.

RADIOACTIVITY

There are more than 100 kinds of atoms. Each is a pure chemical substance or element, such as the hard metal iron or the invisible gas oxygen. Most kinds of atoms are stable, which means they do not change on their own, spontaneously. But a few kinds are unstable. As they change into other types of atoms, they give off or radiate energy – radioactivity.

Henri Becquerel (1852–1908).

THE ATOM AND RADIOACTIVITY

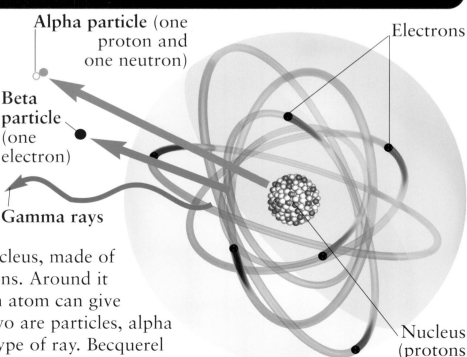

Alpha particle (one proton and one neutron)

Beta particle (one electron)

Gamma rays

Electrons

Nucleus (protons and neutrons)

An atom has a central part, the nucleus, made of particles called protons and neutrons. Around it whizz more particles, electrons. An atom can give off three forms of radioactivity. Two are particles, alpha and beta. The third, gamma, is a type of ray. Becquerel first noticed radioactivity from the substance uranium.

A DANGEROUS MYSTERY

Radioactivity was discovered in 1896 by the French scientist Henri Becquerel. Fellow scientist Marie Curie invented its new name. At first radioactivity was a mystery – invisible but powerful. But its dangers soon became clear as people who worked with radioactive substances fell ill, and some died.

More research by scientists such as Albert Einstein gave a better understanding of this type of energy. From about 1920, people began to wonder if it could be harnessed in some way, perhaps for electrical power.

Radioactivity cannot be seen, heard, smelled, tasted or felt. It must be detected by special sensing equipment like the geiger counter, invented by German scientist Hans Geiger in 1908.

Albert Einstein (1879–1955) made huge advances in science. In 1905 he suggested that matter – a physical object like an atom – could change into pure energy. Also, the reverse could happen, as energy became a solid object. Other scientists were baffled but soon accepted the strange new ideas.

New DISCOVERY

Polish-born French scientist Marie Curie studied Becquerel's 'new energy'. She purified the metals uranium and thorium and showed that they gave off some radioactivity. She also discovered two new chemical elements from their radioactivity alone, naming them polonium and radium.

Marie Curie (1867–1934).

SPLITTING THE 'ATOM'

Nuclear power is named because its energy comes from breaking apart, or splitting, the central piece of an atom – the nucleus.

BROKEN APART

Atoms were thought to be the smallest of all particles, and impossible to split. In 1919, scientist Ernest Rutherford and his team announced that they had broken one apart! In fact, they had split the nucleus of an atom, and energy had been released.

The 1940s–50s saw test 'atom-splitters' like this one at Hanford, Washington, USA. Hanford soon became a major nuclear site.

Green ISSUES

In the 1950s most power stations and factory chimneys burned fossil fuels such as coal and oil. Their smoke and fumes filled the air. Nuclear energy was a great hope, because it would not give off polluting smoke and fumes. But at the time, the various problems of nuclear power were not clear.

1950s: Could nuclear energy bring back blue skies?

CHAIN REACTIONS

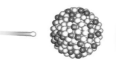

A chain reaction is 'kick-started' by a small amount of energy, then it is self-sustaining (continues on its own). A fast-moving particle like a neutron hits a nucleus, making it come apart. Another neutron is released to continue the process. Heat energy is also released. The original nucleus and its atom have now changed or 'decayed' into the atom of another substance.

SPLIT, SPLIT, SPLIT, SPLIT ...

What if the particles and energy given off by splitting a nucleus could be used to split another nucleus? Then a series, or chain, of reactions would carry on as long as there were suitable nuclei to split, like those of uranium. In 1942 in Chicago, USA, Enrico Fermi carried out the first controlled nuclear chain reaction. The the way was open for nuclear power.

Italian-born Enrico Fermi (1901–54) led the first 'chain reaction' team.

At each stage, nuclei of uranium are hit by neutron particles. They split, giving off heat plus other forms of energy, and more neutrons.

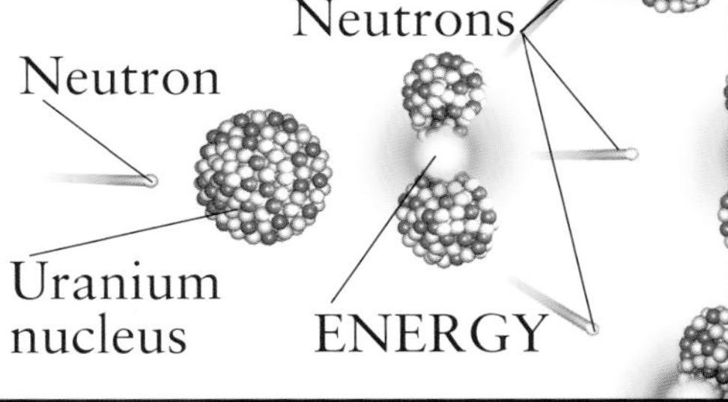

Neutrons

Neutron

Uranium nucleus

ENERGY

9

The main fuel for nuclear power stations is uranium. Pure uranium is a silvery, shiny, hard, heavy metal. It is spread out in the Earth in rocks called ores.

URANIUM ORE

The chief ore of uranium is known as pitchblende. However, the uranium itself is so scattered through this rock, that it takes a house-sized pile of pitchblende to provide a fist-sized lump of uranium.

Spread out through the rocks, uranium's natural radioactivity is not very strong. But at surface mines it can be exposed in leftover waste piles.

FROM ROCK TO ROD

Different types of uranium ore are purified in various ways. They may be ground into powder, floated in tanks to separate heavy and light parts, dissolved and centrifuged – twirled around very fast, like a spin-dryer.

Gradually useful uranium-235 is separated for the nuclear reactor. Care is taken as the uranium becomes more pure and its natural radioactivity more powerful. Plutonium fuel is prepared differently (see page 15).

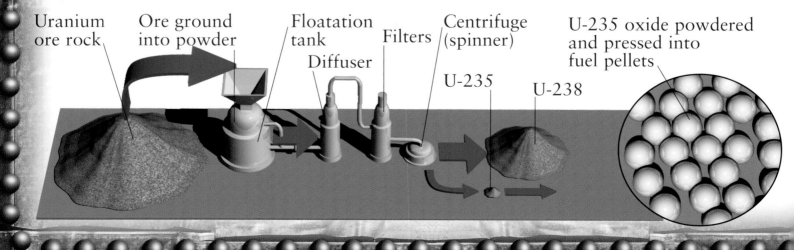

Uranium ore rock

Ore ground into powder

Floatation tank

Diffuser

Filters

Centrifuge (spinner)

U-235

U-238

U-235 oxide powdered and pressed into fuel pellets

Green ISSUES

Mine tunnels deep in the ground have been used to store radioactive wastes from the nuclear industry, after the uranium or other ores have been removed. But water trickling through the rocks can release and transport the radioactivity to threaten wide areas.

Radioactivity: out in ore, back as waste.

URANIUM-235

Purifying uranium from its ore is a difficult process with many physical and chemical stages. Also, not all of this uranium is useful for nuclear power. Like many elements (pure substances), uranium exists in several forms, called isotopes. These look similar, but have slightly different numbers of particles in their atoms. The useful isotope of uranium, U-235, must be separated from the much more common U-238, before it can be used as nuclear fuel.

Fuel pellets are packed into a fuel rod (fuel pin) about 4m long and as wide as a finger.

Up to 200 fuel rods plus a similar number of control rods make up a fuel assembly (fuel element).

A fuel assembly is prepared for the power station reactor.

11

Most power stations burn fuel, to create heat, to boil water into steam, to spin turbines, to turn a generator, to make electricity.

No BURN

A nuclear power station has two main differences from other power stations. First, it does not 'burn' fuel. The heat comes from a controlled chain reaction inside the reactor vessel, which is like a 'nuclear kettle'. Second, the main part of the power station is covered by a giant dome, to keep in any radioactivity that might leak out or escape by accident.

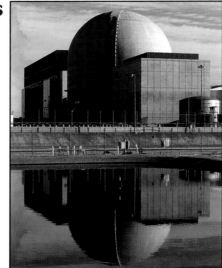

Concrete covers are 'containment' vessels to hold in any hazardous radioactive leaks.

Many parts of the nuclear power station are similar to other big power plants. An energy source boils water into superheated steam, which blasts at enormous pressure along pipes, to the turbines and generators. But the energy source here is radioactive fuel in the reactor vessel. Apart from the usual power station hazards of great temperatures and pressures, an added danger is reactor radioactivity and the radioactive wastes it creates. (Types of reactors are shown on pages 14–15.)

The central control room.

Control room
Fuel loading area

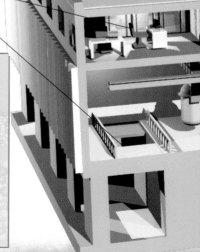

Green **ISSUES**

The radioactivity that provides the basic energy for the power station can spread into many parts, even the cooling water, which is then emptied through pipes into the sea.

Weak radioactivity seeps into the sea.

REACTOR CIRCUITS

Two sets of fluid each have their own circuit. The primary fluid flows through the reactor and gathers heat but also some radioactivity. The secondary fluid collects the heat, as steam, but not the radioactivity.

TURBINE-GENERATOR

High-pressure steam or a similar secondary fluid pushes against the angled blades of a turbine, which turns the electricity generator.

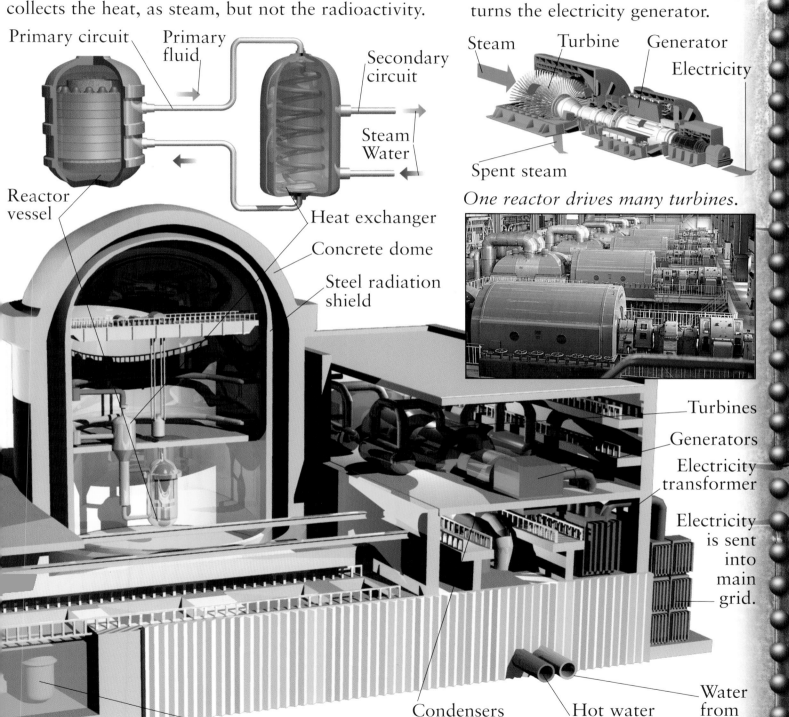

Primary circuit

Primary fluid

Secondary circuit

Steam
Water

Reactor vessel

Heat exchanger

Concrete dome

Steel radiation shield

Steam   Turbine   Generator

Electricity

Spent steam

One reactor drives many turbines.

Turbines

Generators

Electricity transformer

Electricity is sent into main grid.

Fuel storage with coolants and radioactivity shields

Condensers change steam into hot water.

Hot water to cooling towers

Water from cooling towers

Most nuclear reactors work in the same basic way. They control the splitting of nuclei in uranium atoms, which gives off heat. But reactors differ in their shapes and designs.

KEEPING CONTROL

In the reactor, uranium nuclei break, releasing neutrons in a chain reaction. To stop this getting out of hand, control rods absorb or soak up spare neutrons, so that one split nucleus produces only one neutron for the next split. Control rods are usually made of boron. A moderator substance may also be used, to slow neutrons to the most suitable speed.

In a PWR, pressurized water reactor, the sealed primary circuit contains water under great pressure, which stops it boiling. It flows past the fuel assemblies in the reactor core, where it absorbs heat and radioactivity. It then flows around the primary circuit, giving up heat (but not radioactivity) to the secondary circuit, which boils its own water into steam.

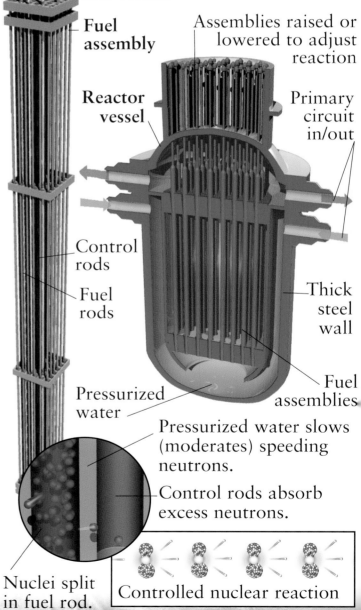

Fuel assembly

Assemblies raised or lowered to adjust reaction

Reactor vessel

Primary circuit in/out

Control rods

Fuel rods

Thick steel wall

Fuel assemblies

Pressurized water

Pressurized water slows (moderates) speeding neutrons.

Control rods absorb excess neutrons.

Nuclei split in fuel rod.

Controlled nuclear reaction

The reactor is hidden under the main dome.

THE FAST-BREEDER

Fuel assembly

Primary circuit of hot sodium out

Upper neutron shield

U-238

Primary circuit of hot sodium out

Core of U-235 or Pu-239

Side neutron shield

U-238

Fast-breeders give off heat, and also use some energy released to make or 'breed' more fuel. A core of Pu-239 (plutonium-239) or U-235 is used to create heat and larger amounts of neutrons. These extra neutrons react with U-238 and turn it into Pu-239. After reprocessing the Pu-239 can be used as fuel in a fast-breeder. The primary fluid is liquid sodium.

Reactor vessel

Control rods

Cool sodium in

Cool sodium   *Tsuroga fast-breeder, Japan.*

Terrorism ISSUES

Uranium, plutonium and similar substances are not only used in power stations. In different forms, they are also used to make nuclear weapons. All nuclear sites must be constantly on guard against terrorists or others, who might try to steal these substances for weapon-making.

Police guard a nuclear storage site.

MOST COMMON TYPES

Many designs of nuclear reactor have been tried, with names such as magnox, light-water, heavy-water and AGC (advanced gas-cooled). The main differences between them are in the make-up of the various fuel rods, control rods and moderators, and the types of fluids in the circuits. About two-thirds of the world's nuclear power stations today have the PWR design.

A lump of uranium, as nuclear fuel, releases more than two million times as much energy as burning a same-sized lump of coal. Why is nuclear power not used more?

PLUS POINTS

Nuclear energy has several benefits. It produces immense power from tiny amounts of fuel. These fuels will last far longer than fossil fuels such as coal, oil and gas, burned in other power stations. Also, burning fossil fuel leads to greenhouse gases that cause global warming, and chemical pollution such as smog and acid rain. Nuclear power produces hardly any of these problems.

Some nuclear wastes are stored in caves or tunnels deep under the sea bed. But earthquakes could crack the rocks, leaking the radioactivity.

Nuclear energy workers wear special suits and masks, which become contaminated as 'low level' waste.

Used nuclear fuel rods and other reactor equipment, and materials from making nuclear weapons, are 'high level' nuclear wastes. Large amounts are stored at Hanford, USA.

MINUS POINTS

However, nuclear energy has several huge drawbacks. One is that it produces great amounts of contaminated wastes – that is, substances and objects that are radioactive, and so dangerous. The radioactivity will last hundreds and even thousands of years. The wastes are stored for now. But no one knows how to make them completely safe, or where to put them safely, for the future.

Green ISSUES

Some low level nuclear waste, which has limited radioactivity, has been dumped into the sea, sealed in barrels or similar containers. But sea water can eat through the containers and allow the dangerous radioactivity to seep out.

A Greenpeace protest against dumping at sea.

OUT OF SIGHT – BUT SAFE?

Burying nuclear waste seems one answer. A possible US site is Yucca Mountain, in the deserts of Nevada. The land is not likely to be disturbed by volcanoes, earthquakes or floods. About 12,000 huge steel-and-glass canisters would be buried 300 metres below the surface.

Yucca Mountain

Storage tunnels

Access tunnels

Canister

High level wastes

Train delivers canisters.

Transporter carries canisters into tunnels.

ACCIDENT PRONE?

Despite endless safety precautions, accidents happen. They even happen in the energy industry. But two features of nuclear power could make a local tragedy into a world disaster.

RADIOACTIVE RELEASE

One problem is the release of radioactivity (radiation). This could pass into air, rivers or seas and spread thousands of kilometres. Even in small amounts it can slowly harm wildlife, crops, farm animals and people. In large amounts it kills in days, even hours.

Truth ISSUES

Nuclear companies often assure the public that any radioactivity they release is tiny. But occasionally, when a level is actually measured, it is not. Some people have come to distrust nuclear industry information.

Power station cooling water: radioactive?

For two days at the Three Mile Island site, there were fears of a reactor meltdown. The problem was contained with no radiation leak or loss of life. But then came news of a cover-up.

In 1986, a reactor exploded at Chernobyl, Ukraine. The containment roof blasted off, releasing radioactivity across Europe. Thousands of people fled, and some later died. The reactor was finally sealed in a concrete 'coffin' (inset).

MELTDOWN!

A second possible problem is that a power station's chain reaction gets out of control. It speeds up, releasing more radioactivity and heat. If a reactor got too hot, it would melt. If it happened very suddenly, the result would be like a nuclear bomb.

Radioactivity gets into soil, plants, animals and people.

NUCLEAR CRISES

In 1979 Harrisburg, the capital of Pennsylvania, USA, became the focus of world attention. A nuclear power station nearby, at Three Mile Island (left), suffered a series of faults. An explosion was narrowly avoided. Seven years later a Chernobyl reactor was not quite so fortunate (above and right). Again, a sequence of problems occurred. Cooling equipment failed, then the back-up safety versions failed too. The final explosion blew radioactivity into the atmosphere to drift over Europe and East Asia.

2 Back-up cooling system fails.

3 Pressure of explosion breaks inner and outer domes.

4 Radioactive dust and gas spread vast distances.

5 Reactor vessel overheats and melting fuel escapes.

1 Cooling system pipe breaks and leaks.

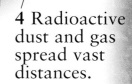

THE WEAPONS LINK

A nuclear chain reaction can be slow and controlled, as in a power station. Or it can happen in a few seconds, making the biggest explosion ever.

WMDs

Nuclear or atomic weapons are known as WMDs, weapons of mass destruction. They could flatten great cities, spread deadly radioactivity over whole continents and kill millions. They have only been used in warfare twice, in Japan in 1945, at the end of World War Two. But eight nations around the world keep them on standby, with occasional tests. Others hope to possess them in the near future.

Green ISSUES

The world has enough nuclear weapons to destroy all life, several times. The 1950s–60s 'arms race' saw more and more built. From the 1970s the numbers have slowly fallen. World leaders like George Bush (USA) and Vladimir Putin (Russia) continue to agree these arms reductions or limits.

Putin (left) and Bush, 2001.

Perhaps the most sinister nuclear weapons are missiles such as Trident, fired from submarines unseen and almost undetectable, beneath the waves. These submarines are 'double nuclear', being driven by nuclear power plants (see page 24).

The first atomic weapon fell on Hiroshima, Japan, in August 1945. Up to 100,000 people died at once.

A test nuclear explosion in the Pacific forms the typical 'mushroom' cloud.

TYPES OF WEAPONS

In an atom bomb (A-bomb), pieces of uranium or plutonium are smashed together by a small explosion, to start a chain reaction. In the hydrogen bomb (H-bomb) the energy comes not from splitting nuclei, which is called nuclear fission, but by joining them – nuclear fusion.

THE H-BOMB

There are several types of H-bombs, which are about 1,000 times more powerful than A-bombs. Some use the forms, or isotopes, of hydrogen called H-2 (deuterium) and H-3 (tritium). Their nuclei fuse with explosive energy.

H-2

H-3

Metal cores

Uranium casing

Fusion chain reaction

If nuclear weapons fell into terrorist hands, the world could be held to ransom. Such weapons are heavily guarded. So are the raw materials that could be used to make them.

21

The nuclear industry is much more than bombs and power stations. Nuclear energy is used in various ways, from scientific research and exploring space to helping the sick.

RECYCLING

After fuel rods are used in a typical nuclear reactor, they may still contain useful energy and substances. The rods are 'reprocessed', which is similar to recycling. The useful substances include rare metals. These form as by-products of the chain reaction and can be purified for research and industry.

Used fuel rods (inset) may be taken to a reprocessing centre for various types of recycling. But there are only a few such centres. Protesters say that any transport of nuclear material is dangerous; an accident will happen.

Green **ISSUES**

Radioactivity is known to cause diseases such as leukaemias (types of blood cancer). People who work or live near nuclear sites are often surveyed to see if diseases are more common there. The results can lead to huge arguments.

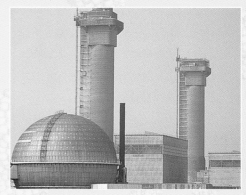

A danger to people nearby?

Nuclear material on its way to and from reprocessing is a possible target for weapon-makers and arms dealers. Some nuclear cargoes are sent halfway round the world.

ENRICHING

Used or spent nuclear fuel can be enriched, which makes it more concentrated and ready to go back into a reactor. But other types of reprocessing yield 'weapons grade' uranium or plutonium for bombs and missiles.

A whole area of identifying and treating illness is known as nuclear medicine. Tiny, safe amounts of radioactive tracer substances are put into the body and followed with special cameras or sensors. The way that a tracer passes through body parts reveals certain illnesses. More powerful radioactivity, or radiation, can be used to kill growths or tumours, as when treating cancer.

In nuclear imaging, also called radionuclide scanning, a person is given a radioactive substance, by swallowing or injection as a drip-feed.

GAMMA CAMERA SCANNER

The radioactive tracer in a patient gives off weak gamma rays. These hit crystals on a plate in the camera and make tiny flashes of light. Sensors detect the flashes and send signals to a computer to build up the picture.

Sensors send signals to computer.

Flash (scintillation)

Light-sensitive crystals on plate

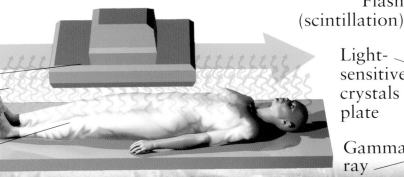

Gamma camera

Gamma rays

Patient with radioactive (radio-isotope) tracer

Gamma ray

It's very difficult to move a nuclear power station. But small mobile or portable nuclear power plants have uses – from deep sea to deep space.

CRITICAL MASS

A nuclear power plant has size limits. There should be enough of its fuel for a chain reaction to start and continue. This amount is called 'critical mass' and varies according to the fuel, from pea- to car-sized.

Green ISSUES

In 2000, the Russian nuclear submarine *Kursk* sank in the Barents Sea of the cold north. There were immediate worries that water would leak into the craft and release radioactivity – from both the nuclear power plant and the *Granit* nuclear missiles.

Nuclear power suits submarines (below). It uses little fuel, and unlike a diesel or gas turbine, it needs no oxygen for burning, with no exhaust. A nuclear sub can stay under for months.

Kursk *wrecked, 118 lost.*

Nuclear fuel is tiny for its energy content. Icebreaker Vaygach *carries enough for years at sea – as the protesters show.*

TOO HEAVY TO FLY

Another limit is not the reactor but its container. This is usually a thick metal casing or shield, to keep in radioactivity. It is far too heavy for any plane!

Weight is less important at sea. Various ships have nuclear power, including icebreakers and submarines. Radioactivity does not matter for unmanned space probes. Small nuclear plants can generate electricity for years, from a fist-sized lump of fuel.

The US Voyager *deep-space probes, launched in 1977, each had a plutonium-fuelled nuclear reactor (in the shiny three-part cylinder at the upper left).*

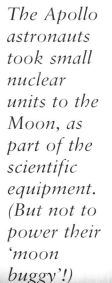

The Apollo astronauts took small nuclear units to the Moon, as part of the scientific equipment. (But not to power their 'moon buggy'!)

NUCLEAR FUSION

The biggest amounts of nuclear energy are not produced by huge power stations or nuclear weapons. They are far away in space – stars.

FUSION FURNACE

Our world is warm and bright thanks to nuclear energy from our nearest star, the Sun. In a star, heat, light and other forms of energy are made by nuclear fusion.

Fusion is similar but 'opposite' to fission. Two nuclei (centres of atoms) merge at incredible temperature and pressure. The result is a single nucleus of a different substance, plus fast-moving particles like neutrons and immense amounts of heat and other energy. Several test fusion reactors have been built. But practical fusion power, for electricity, is years away.

Fusion reactors have a hollow ring shape like a doughnut – a torus or 'tokomak'. The gas-like plasma inside is so hot, about 100 million degrees Celsius, that no solid substance can stand it. Powerful magnets in the walls keep the plasma in the middle of the space, touching nothing.

Green ISSUES

In stars, the nuclei of hydrogen atoms fuse in a process called the 'proton-proton reaction'. Here on Earth, the benefits of a fusion reactor for making electricity could be very little nuclear waste with greatly reduced radioactivity, and almost endless fuel that the reactor makes for itself.

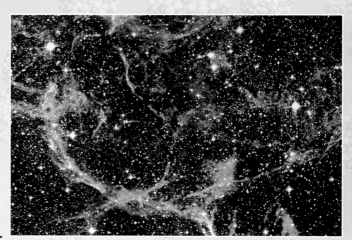

Stars are massive 'fusion furnaces' far in space.

Conditions inside the reactor are closely checked during a test run. So far, only brief bursts of fusion have occurred, with far more energy put in than comes out.

THE 'TOKOMAK'

A fusion reactor uses two forms or isotopes of hydrogen, H-2 and H-3 (see page 21). They are made so hot that they change from gas to plasma, when electrons come away from their nuclei. Two 'naked nuclei' join to make a new nucleus, of helium, plus a neutron and energy. The heat is soaked up by a 'blanket' of the substance lithium around the plasma.

The gases inside the reactor are heated so much that they are no longer gases. They change into another form of matter known as plasma.

H-3 (tritium)

H-2 (deuterium)

Nuclei fuse

Neutron released

Lithium blanket

Plasma space

Fuel inlet

Inner ring of magnets

Plasma exhaust

Outer ring of magnets

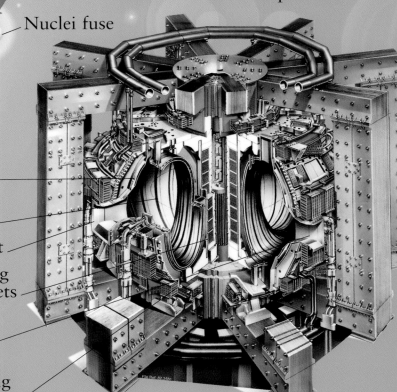

NO TO NUCLEAR?

'NO NUKES!' chant demonstrators and protesters. But the arguments about nuclear weapons and nuclear power are not always crystal clear.

BALANCE OF POWER

Supporters of nuclear weapons might say that because some nations have them, this helps to keep the peace. The terrifying idea of nuclear conflict holds everyone back from starting a war. A reply is: destroy all nuclear weapons, to remove the threat of such world disaster in the first place.

Is the nuclear industry run well? Opponents point to common and continuing examples of leaks, breaks, faults and 'human error'.

Crosses honour Chernobyl victims. Harm spread across many nations, poor and rich. Radioactivity respects no borders.

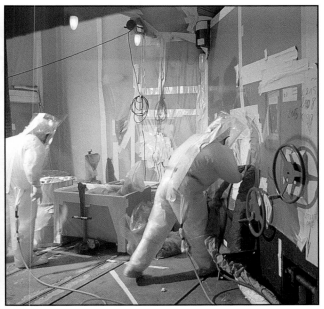
CND, *the Campaign for Nuclear Disarmament, began in the 1950s to prevent the prospect of nuclear war.*

Green ISSUES

Rising radioactivity is found in many places – in the sea, at the poles, in deserts and on high mountains. Some of it came from test explosions years ago. Some is more recent. No one knows if this radioactivity is causing slow, long-term damage to the natural world.

Warning: who would eat radioactive fish?

Nuclear power may seem inexpensive. But old reactors need millions to 'decommission' and make safer.

NUCLEAR ENERGY

A radioactivity-release accident at a nuclear power station might devastate vast areas, ruin the lives of millions and destroy nature. Even without an accident, giant piles of nuclear waste collect daily, with no plan to make them completely safe.

Nuclear supporters say that our main power fuels – coal, gas, oil – are running out. They cause air pollution, global warming, rising sea levels and flooded cities. It's a difficult choice.

29

Some nuclear power stations (here in Bulgaria) have been partly built, then left due to lack of money and public protest.

Worldwide, about 420 nuclear power stations produce one-tenth of all our electricity. Some nations plan more nuclear power. Others have banned it.

THE WAY AHEAD

Each region tries to balance its energy supplies against its own needs and resources. If a country has no oil, gas or coal, but it does have nuclear fuel, and the technology to build nuclear power stations, then perhaps this is an option, for now. But problems remain such as radioactive waste, possible accident, public opposition and protest. Many people believe that the future lies in using more energy from renewable or sustainable sources, like wind and sunshine, and at the same time, using less energy all round.

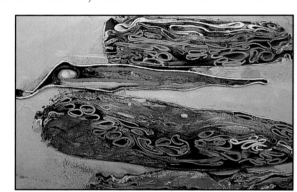

Nuclear waste may be dumped at sea, buried or even sealed in glass (above). But it's not going away.

SAFER NUCLEAR POWER?

Top-up tube
Primary circuit
Emergency boron-water intakes
Boron-rich water

Uranium reactor
Steam to turbines
Cooled water
Heat exchanger

New designs for the nuclear industry aim to make the whole process safer, while producing less radioactive waste. In this version the nuclear reactor is in a giant tank of water containing the substance boron, which slows or stops the chain reaction. If a fault occurs, the boron-rich water automatically floods the reactor and nuclear fission ceases.

GLOSSARY

chain reaction

A process that, once started, continues to happen by itself, without needing extra energy. In a nuclear chain reaction, nuclei split apart, causing others to do the same, and so on.

decommission

In the nuclear industry, to make an old power station, fuel processing site, or other place where there are dangerous substances and radioactivity, safe for the future.

global warming

The rise in temperature all around the world, due to greenhouse gases (see below) in the layer of air, or atmosphere. They trap extra amounts of the Sun's heat.

greenhouse gases

Substances in the atmosphere (air) which hold in or retain the Sun's heat. They keep it near to Earth's surface, rather than letting it escape into space, causing global warming (see above).

nucleus

The central part of an atom (which is the smallest piece or unit of a substance). A nucleus is usually made of two types of particles, called protons and neutrons.

radioactivity

An invisible form of energy given off by certain substances, such as some forms of uranium and plutonium. There are three kinds. Alpha and beta radioactivity are particles, gamma radioactivity is rays (gamma rays).

renewable

A process or substance that is sustainable and can continue for a very long time, using raw materials or resources that are recycled or made again.

turbine

A shaft (central rod or axle) with a circle of angled blades, like a fan. These spin around when steam or another high-pressure substance blows past them.

31